W9-BMU-770

Countries
We Come
From

South Korea

by Jessica Rudolph

Consultants:

Marjorie Faulstich Orellana, PhD
Professor of Urban Schooling
University of California, Los Angeles

Hye-Young Kwon
University of Southern California
Los Angeles, California

BEARPORT
PUBLISHING

New York, New York

Publisher: Kenn Goin
Editor: Jessica Rudolph
Creative Director: Spencer Brinker
Design: Debrah Kaiser
Photo Researcher: Olympia Shannon

Library of Congress Cataloging-in-Publication Data

Rudolph, Jessica.
    South Korea / by Jessica Rudolph.
        pages cm. — (Countries we come from)
    Includes bibliographical references and index.
    Audience: Ages 4–8.
    ISBN 978-1-62724-854-9 (library binding) — ISBN 1-62724-854-4 (library binding)
    1. Korea (South)—Juvenile literature. I. Title.
    DS907.4.R83 2016
    951.95—dc23
                                            2015004743

For more information, write to Bearport Publishing Company, Inc., 45 West 21st Street, Suite 3B, New York, New York 10010. Printed in the United States of America.

10 9 8 7 6 5 4 3 2 1

Contents

This Is South Korea

BUSY

Beautiful

Ancient

South Korea is a country in Asia.

More than 50 million people live there.

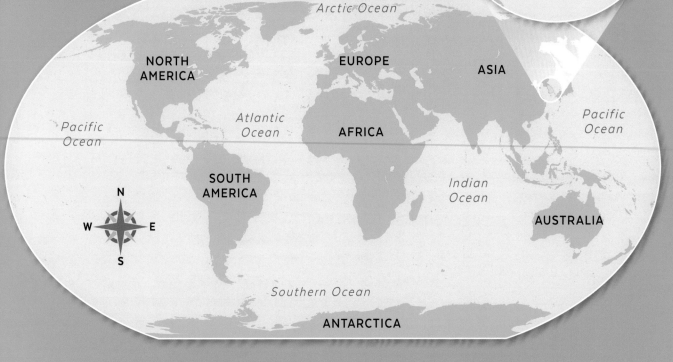

South Korea

Arctic Ocean

NORTH AMERICA

EUROPE

ASIA

Pacific Ocean

Atlantic Ocean

AFRICA

Pacific Ocean

SOUTH AMERICA

Indian Ocean

N
W   E
S

AUSTRALIA

Southern Ocean

ANTARCTICA

Most of South Korea is surrounded by water.

South Korea has different types of land.

There are mountains, islands, and beaches.

South Korea has more than 3,000 islands.

There are many national parks in South Korea.

The plants and animals that live in them are **protected**.

Seoraksan National Park

Deer, bears, and many kinds of birds live in the parks.

South Korea has a long history.

People have lived there for 5,000 years.

Long ago, rulers built **palaces** and **temples**.

Today, people can visit many of the old buildings.

Gyeongbokgung Palace

興禮門

13

Korean is the main language
of South Korea.

In Korean, the word for *yes* is:

Ye (YEH)

The word for *no* is:

Aniyo (ah-nee-YO)

정지
STOP

Korean letters look very different from English letters.

Most South Koreans live in cities. **Skyscrapers** rise above the streets.

Fast trains carry people from city to city.

Some trains travel 185 miles per hour (298 kph)!

Seoul is South Korea's largest city.

It's also the country's **capital**.

Seoul is one of the largest cities in the world. About ten million people live there.

A worker building a car

20

Many South Koreans work in large factories.

Some people make cars or phones.

South Korean products are sold all over the world.

Many South Koreans work as farmers.

They grow rice in wet fields.

Other people catch food in the ocean.

People catch fish, octopuses, lobsters, and shrimp.

Korean food is known for its delicious flavors.

Many meals include rice, tea, and kimchi.

Kimchi can be made with different vegetables and spices.

Families often sit on the floor during meals. Food is served on low tables.

South Koreans play many sports, such as soccer.

In South Korea, soccer is called football.

Another popular sport is tae kwon do (TEYE KWAHN DOH). It's a **martial art** that began in South Korea.

South Koreans celebrate many holidays.

One important holiday is the Lunar New Year, or Seollal.

Koreans often wear traditional clothes, called hanbok, during holidays.

People celebrate Seollal with their families.

Fast Facts

Capital city: Seoul

Population of South Korea: More than 50 million

Main language: Korean

Money: Won

Major religions: Christianity, Buddhism

Neighboring Country: North Korea

Cool Fact: Jeju Island is famous for its female divers. The divers gather seaweed, octopuses, and oysters. The women don't use any breathing equipment when they go deep under the water.

capital (KAP-uh-tuhl) the city where a country's government is based

martial art (MAR-shuhl ART) a form of self-defense, such as karate or judo, that comes from Asia

palaces (PAL-iss-iz) grand homes of kings, queens, emperors, or other rulers

protected (proh-TEK-tid) kept safe from harm

skyscrapers (SKYE-skray-purz) very tall buildings

temples (TEM-puhlz) religious buildings where people come to pray

31

Index

Read More

Miller, Jennifer A. *South Korea (Country Explorers).* Minneapolis, MN: Lerner (2010).

Walters, Tara. *South Korea (True Book).* New York: Children's Press (2008).

Learn More Online

To learn more about South Korea, visit **www.bearportpublishing.com/CountriesWeComeFrom**

About the Author

Jessica Rudolph lives in Connecticut. She has edited and written many books about history, science, and nature for children.